CHILDREN NEED
HOMES

Harry Undy

Wayland

THE WORLD'S CHILDREN

Children Need Education
Children Need Families
Children Need Food
Children Need A Future
Children Need Health Care
Children Need Homes
Children Need Recreation
Children Need Water

Book Editor: Amanda Earl
Series Editor: Stephen White-Thomson
Consultant: Save the Children
Picture Editor: Amanda Earl

All words that appear in **bold** in the text
are explained in the glossary on page 44.

First published in 1988 by
Wayland (Publishers) Limited
61 Western Road, Hove
East Sussex BN3 1JD, England

British Library Cataloguing in Publication Data
Undy, Harry,
  Children need homes – (The World's Children)
  1. Homeless children
  I. Title
  362,7'044

  ISBN 1 85210 105 9

Phototypeset by Kalligraphics Ltd, Redhill, Surrey
Printed by G. Canale & C.S.p.A., Turin
Bound by Casterman S.A., Belgium

Front cover: Brazilian children outside their
newly built house in Olinda.

Back cover: Different homes suit different
climates. Here, a grandfather and his family sit
outside their home on stilts in Papua New Guinea.

Title page: All children of all races need a home to
live in.

Contents page: In the rainforests of Ecuador,
homes are usually made from giant leaves.

CONTENTS

THE RIGHTS OF THE CHILD

Eglantine Jebb, the founder of The Save the Children Fund, drafted the Rights of the Child in 1923. It was revised in 1948 by the present Declaration of the Rights of the Child, commonly known as the Declaration of Geneva. These principles form the basis of our work and the Charter of The Save the Children Fund.

1 The Child must be protected beyond and above all considerations of race, nationality or creed.

2 The Child must be cared for with due respect for the family as an entity.

3 The Child must be given the means requisite for its normal development, materially, morally and spiritually.

4 The Child that is hungry must be fed, the child that is sick must be nursed, the child that is mentally or physically handicapped must be helped, the maladjusted child must be re-educated, the orphan and the waif must be sheltered and succoured.

5 The Child must be the first to receive relief in time of distress.

6 The Child must enjoy the full benefits provided by social welfare and social security schemes, must receive a training which will enable it, at the right time, to earn a livelihood, and must be protected against every form of exploitation.

7 The Child must be brought up in the consciousness that its talents must be devoted to the service of its fellow men.

FOREWORD BY HRH THE PRINCESS ROYAL PRESIDENT OF SAVE THE CHILDREN

BUCKINGHAM PALACE

All children, regardless of race, nationality or creed, have basic rights. These rights were outlined by Eglantine Jebb, the founder of Save the Children, in 1923 and they have now become an integral part of the United Nations charter. You can read them on the opposite page.

I welcome this thought-provoking series and applaud the way it confronts the issues facing today's children throughout the world. In the end we are all part of the same human race, and not so different from one another. Where differences do exist, they enrich us.

As Britain's largest international children's charity, Save the Children works where there is real need, both in the UK and in over 50 countries around the world. The idea behind all our projects is to encourage people to help themselves. But SCF also accepts its responsibility to talk about the issues of world-wide child poverty - particularly to the young - which makes this work so necessary. This series is designed to do just that.

I am sure that this colourful series will be an invaluable resource for any school whose aim is to make their pupils think beyond the confines of their playground and their community. We are one world after all. Let's try and be one.

Anne

HOME: MORE THAN A SHELTER

Every child needs a home, a place which is more than just a shelter from the world outside. Every home is different and we will see how people all over the world have made homes which suit their way of life and the country they live in. Different needs demand all kinds of solutions; a home to protect you from the heat, will not be like a home which keeps out the cold; in the same way, a shelter in a busy town will not be the same as a shelter for a traveller in a rainforest.

A child's home should do much to provide good health and happiness, as well as be a shelter from danger. To grow up safely, protection from enemies, including dangerous people, animals and viruses, is important. Fresh air, light and space to move are important, too.

Happiness and peace of mind also depends on people, so a good home should provide care, good company, and, most importantly, love and security. There are many problems in the world that make this difficult, such as poverty, illness, **unemployment**, lack of education and **racism**. So, you see it takes more than a sound roof and strong walls to make a good home.

◁ In north-east Brazil, this family will be cool and dry in their house built of local mud, bricks and grass.

Half a world away, in Indonesia, houses are built on stilts to suit the tropical climate. ▽

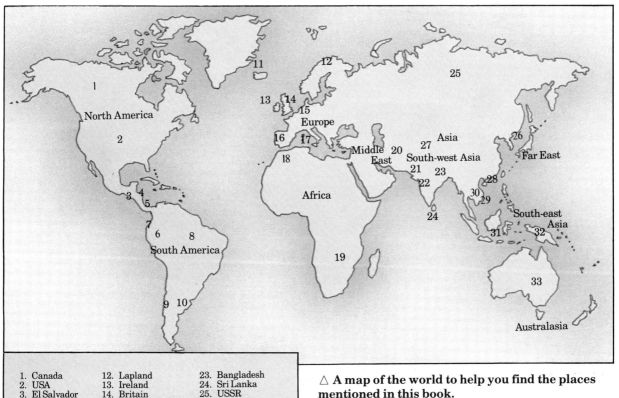

1. Canada	12. Lapland	23. Bangladesh
2. USA	13. Ireland	24. Sri Lanka
3. El Salvador	14. Britain	25. USSR
4. Honduras	15. West Germany	26. South Korea
5. Nicaragua	16. Spain	27. Tibet (Xizang)
6. Colombia	17. Italy	28. Hong Kong
7. Ecuador	18. Morocco	29. Vietnam
8. Brazil	19. Zimbabwe	30. Kampuchea
9. Chile	20. Afghanistan	31. Indonesia
10. Argentina	21. Pakistan	32. Papua New Guinea
11. Iceland	22. India	33. Australia

△ **A map of the world to help you find the places mentioned in this book.**

This Lapp family have to rebuild their home each time they move to follow the reindeer migration in Spring. ▽

When you look at the homes of people around the world, think about where they are and what they are for. In countries where there are good roads, travelling people can use a home on wheels; but people who travel with reindeer in Lapland, for instance, where there are few roads, have learned how to build a good hut every time they stop. The large windows, open doorways and wide verandahs of tropical homes would not be suitable for life in a cold climate, where double glazing, draught excluders and roof insulation are essential.

So, whatever the outside of a home looks like, think about the people inside. Homes are for people.

7

HOMELESS CHILDREN

For many children in the world, their home is on the streets of a big city. The exact number of these 'street children' is not known, but there are millions of them. The greatest number are found in the large, growing cities of the developing world – Mexico City, Rio de Janeiro in Brazil, Seoul in South Korea, Bombay in India, Buenos Aires in Argentina, for example – not in the capitals of rich nations.

▽ **Family life for thousands in Bombay is open to all eyes. Sleeping, cooking, eating, living and dying is done on the streets with no privacy.**

Life is hard for these children. Some live in gangs to protect each other and share the food, money or clothing they beg, earn or steal. Street gangs fight each other and the children live in constant fear of the police.

Most of these children left home because their families were too poor to feed and care for them. They could not find work on the farms if they were country children, so they made their way to the towns; homeless town children do not go to the country because they know there is nothing for them there.

Living on the streets, they try to sell fruit, newspapers or cigarettes to car drivers; they wash cars, beg, carry suitcases and shopping bags, and steal. Poor people do not lead the same long, healthy lives that most rich people lead, but street children are in greater danger.

Ever since towns began to grow larger, children have been drawn to them. It can take a long time for city councils, or national governments, to provide care and shelter for these children, so sometimes individual people step in to help first. In nineteenth-century London, Dr Thomas Barnardo provided homes for children, and protected them from the punishment they would otherwise get for being troublesome. In Milan, in the middle of this century, Father Borelli set the same example. Now, in the new, rapidly-growing cities of the developing world, the same lesson – the importance of a secure home – is also being learned.

When very young children have no family and no home, special care has to be given, as it was to this Vietnamese baby in an orphanage. ▽

▽ **For more than a hundred years Dr Barnardo's Homes have sheltered homeless children in Britain. This picture, taken in Edinburgh, Scotland in 1912, shows homeless boys waiting for their tea.**

LEAVING HOME

Thousands of people – children, the young and the old – leave their home because they feel unhappy and cannot cope with the pressures it puts on them. They leave in search of a dream. When you are unhappy at home it is easy to believe that somewhere else, anywhere else, could be more exciting and give you more freedom and more money.

The American 'bag lady', with all her possessions in a supermarket trolley, is one picture of this kind of wanderer. In Australia the 'jolly **swagman**' has been replaced by less happy travellers who do not find fame and fortune. Stories of big cities being paved with gold are just fairy tales, but children still go away to seek their fortune.

Jack is a teenager and, although he is English, his experience is similar to that of young people all over the world who decide to leave home. For many of them, however, there is not such a happy end to the story.

There are no benches at Euston Station, but still young homeless people find a place to sleep. ▷

Jack was unhappy at school and was fed up with his home. The television seemed to promise him that there was an easier life somewhere else, if only he could reach it. So, he ran away. He took money and his sports bag, and hid on a train to London. At **Euston Station** he pushed past the ticket collector and ran.

This meant that he did not get in trouble with the police for fare-dodging; but it also meant that the people at Euston who are on the look-out for young people in trouble, did not find him either.

Jack soon found out that things were no better for teenagers in London. A tramp showed him the way to a hostel where he could sleep, but he could not find a job, so his money soon ran out. He swapped his sports bag for a packet of sandwiches and kept his belongings in a plastic carrier bag. Every night he headed for the River Thames and slept in a cardboard box under the arches of one of the bridges over the river.

The bad weather that winter brought him luck. When it snowed, the television cameras came to film the down-and-outs, and Jack's parents saw him, after months of worry.

Jack's father rushed to London to talk to him. Jack was still not sure that he wanted to go home because he hoped his dream might still come true. But he looked at his plastic bag and his cardboard box, and remembered how miserable and frightened he had been every night. So he gave what few belongings he had to the people on the pavement, and went off to try to make his old home a real home.

Cardboard boxes provide little warmth or comfort – this is a common scene around London's embankment. ▷

SPECIAL NEEDS, SPECIAL HOMES

For children who are handicapped, special care is needed. Often this cannot be provided at home. In rich countries, essential services are more easily provided than in poor, war-torn countries. At Khemisset, in Morocco, Save the Children runs a home for handicapped children. Here, the children are given medical treatment and an education which they would not receive at home.

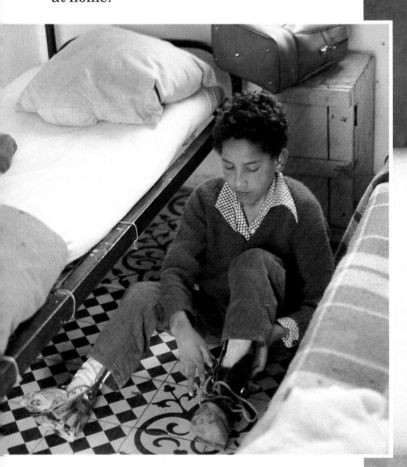

△ At Khemisset this boy shares a dormitory in the Save the Children home. He has learned to get himself ready for school.

When the right help and encouragement are given, children can overcome some of their handicaps and enjoy a special kind of football. ▷

At Khemisset, the primary school is very near to the children's living quarters. ▽

Even in the developed world, it is often difficult for a handicapped person to travel. In Morocco, it would be impossible for a handicapped child to travel even a few kilometres to a school. At Khemisset, all the facilities are close together. There are dormitories close to the primary school, and special buses to take older children to the secondary schools in the town.

Getting medical treatment can be a problem in a country where there are only a few doctors working long distances apart. At Khemisset, there is a **physiotherapist** to give help and treatment, and special arrangements have been made for surgical operations to be performed in Marrakech. There are also workshops making and repairing walking aids.

Save the Children staff do not try to take the place of the real parents, but they do try to help solve some of the problems which affect the handicapped children. So, Khemisset is a very special home for many children, even to those who have succeeded in moving on to continue their lives elsewhere.

13

HIGH-RISE HOUSING

In old Hollywood films, or in American soap operas, we often see people leading rich and glamorous lives in beautiful skyscraper apartments. But we know that in real life, in towns and cities all over the world, life can be dreadful in a high-rise building. Today, many of these tower blocks are being knocked down because we have learned that they are not the answer to housing large numbers of people where space is limited.

▽ This family in Ireland waits for the lift: will it be working? Will it be clean? Will it be safe? There are no doubts for these children in Germany: they know their homes are cared for. ▷

The huge difference between a Hollywood-style skyscraper and an inner-city tower block is due to money. A luxury block has good walls, floors and windows. Rain, wind and noise are kept out, warmth is kept in. The heating system works. The caretaker and porter make sure that the place is safe and that the lifts work. Shared areas of the building, such as the stairs and corridors, are cleaned, carpeted and well lit so that there are no dark corners. The flats are privately owned by people who can afford the maintenance costs.

A cheaply-built block of flats is another story. Rain, wind and noise all get in where they are not wanted, and warmth escapes. The heating system does not often work, but if it does, it is so expensive that the tenants cannot afford to use it fully. This often means that the building becomes damp, and then the bricks and concrete gradually rot away. There is no caretaker or security guard, so children and adults may be attacked and robbed in the lifts or on the landings or stairs. Bare, concrete corridors are dirty and dangerous places, so parents dare not let their children play there.

If there is any greenery growing on a luxury tower block, it will be in a roof or terrace garden. Greenery growing on a tower block may be mould, or weeds growing in a crack in the walls. These flats are usually the homes of much poorer people who have to rely on landlords to keep up the maintenance of the buildings. Parents make great efforts to move their families out of these 'filing cabinets for people', but for many there is no alternative.

So many families live in these flats in Hong Kong that washing hangs from every window. ▷

HOW TO HELP

For a society to be healthy it needs to care for all the people within it who find themselves in trouble, for whatever reason. We expect this from our families and we hope for it among friends.

Finding a home for someone who needs it for a short time can work on a simple 'please help me' basis. If your aunt and uncle's house burned down, your family would find space for them for a day or two, even if it meant that someone had to sleep on the floor! There are also a few charities who will arrange help in this kind of emergency.

For those homeless people who do not have a caring family, society should provide shelter. Children who are badly hurt in their own homes need protection; women who are being beaten by their husbands and have to leave home with their children need shelter and support; families and individuals who are thrown out of their homes because they cannot pay their rent or **mortgage** need care and advice. Homelessness is a worldwide problem and countries have different ways of meeting their own particular needs.

There is another kind of homelessness which steps outside national boundaries. In many countries, such as Chile in South America, Sri Lanka or Indonesia, people risk being injured, killed or imprisoned, not because they are criminals but because they oppose the **policies** of their government. In this situation, people run away for their safety and become **refugees**.

△ (top) In London, whole families are forced to live with all their possessions in one small room.

△ This group from Pakistan arrive at a refugee camp, but they are still worried because they have not yet been told if they can stay.

The United Nations High Commissioner for Refugees has persuaded most governments to agree to accept refugees and not send them back if they are truly at risk. When there is no such agreement, refugees may be **deported** instead of being given **asylum**.

When a country knows that refugees are coming, preparations can be made. These rows of tents in Honduras mean the refugees are protected. ▽

In the USA, there is a movement which gives '**sanctuary**' in churches to Latin American refugees who are likely to be returned to their native country by the American government. The people in the Sanctuary movement know they are breaking the law in helping, but have decided that, whether it is legal or not, the refugees and their children need shelter and eventually a home.

A SENSE OF BELONGING

Homes are often destroyed by natural forces. Bursting dams, swollen rivers, hurricanes, volcanoes and earthquakes are all powers of destruction.

Etna, Stromboli, Fujiyama, St.Helens, Popacatapetl, Pelée, Heimaey and Krakatoa are all active volcanoes. They have all killed people and destroyed communities. The stream of molten lava, flying rocks and gases of an eruption destroy everything in their path.

In the past, when an alarm has been sounded before an eruption, people have refused to leave their homes. Sometimes this is because they did not believe the warning, or because they preferred to die in their homes. With the same feeling of belonging, people return to the slopes of these volcanoes after an eruption, when they are fully aware of the danger.

When they leave their homes as refugees they could plan to live somewhere safer. They could look for a new home where their children could grow up without the same fears. But most of them want to go back.

People love the homes they know. Even if houses are burned or buried, the place is home. But, on a volcano there is another reason to stay. The soil is very rich and so the crops are very good. The farmers eat well and are sure of good prices at the market. Java is a volcanic island the size of New York State, but it supports a population of nearly 60 million – larger than that of Britain.

After San Salvador was hit by an earthquake in 1986, the poorer people had to make their own repairs. For many families, like this one, the work was to build their own home again from the ground up. ▽

So, the slopes of a volcano provide a powerful combination of security and danger, and the communities that live on them feel a strong sense of belonging.

▷ Some destruction is in the name of 'progress'. Soon this Brazilian family will be homeless because a new dam will create a lake over their house and fields.

▽ The volcanic eruption at Heimaey in Iceland had such power that nothing was safe against it. Even well-built homes were destroyed, yet within weeks, the people returned to rebuild their homes.

A COUNTRY IS HOME

The people of Nicaragua in Central America have had a very hard time, being pushed around by more powerful countries. A **guerrilla war** still goes on, with forces supported by the USA on one side and Russia on the other.

For many years, until 1979, the country was ruled by the Somoza family. There were no free elections, so the people could not choose their ruler. President Anastasio Somoza was a brutal dictator who used the armed forces, the police and the civil service to do as he pleased. Many people were put in prison, tortured and killed because they disagreed with him. Many Nicaraguans became **exiles**. Whole families were forced to leave their homeland to find safety abroad because they were terrified.

Hundreds of children became orphans, and others left the country with their parents. While the parents worked, or plotted against Somoza, the children went to school in their place of **refuge**. In this way, they gained an education which many of them probably would not have had at home.

In 1979, after a **civil war** in which 40,000 people died, Somoza was defeated. The Sandinista group, which led the uprising, became the new government. Immediately, most of the political exiles wanted to return home with their families, to help build the new Nicaragua. It had become a poor country, because Somoza had been robbing it for years.

△ The people of El Salvador, like those in Nicaragua, have had to leave their homes and flee from danger. This is what many refugee camps look like.

The new government believed that it was important for the future of Nicaragua that more people could read. In 1980, the newly educated children and young people who had returned home joined in a great **literacy** crusade, which cost $12,000,000. Many schools in the towns were closed so that teachers could go out into the villages where they were needed to lead the work. More than 400,000 people completed the basic reading course. Nicaraguans are proud of the country which is their home.

△ As they continue to battle for their freedom, Nicaragua's new government has encouraged people to learn to read and write. Here, the adults are in the school desks.

Children too have learnt the importance of Nicaragua's literary crusade. ▷

A NEW HOME

During, and after, the Vietnam War well over half a million people left the country to find new homes. The exact total will never be known. Many fled but never reached their destination and died at sea. Even as late as 1986, when over 18,000 people left Vietnam with the government's permission, more than 19,000 left as refugees without permits.

Many of the refugees were children. In wartime, and in the troubled times soon after the war, thousands of children were separated from their parents. Some of the lucky ones found relatives after reaching safety, but many children were quite alone or just with brothers and sisters.

The people of North America, Europe and Australasia who agreed to help these orphaned refugees faced a big question. What kind of home did the children need? Would it be right to send one child at a time to any family ready to accept them? The child would have plenty of love and care, but would he or she be expected to grow up as a young American, European or Australian? Gradually, such children would lose any real understanding or knowledge of *being* Vietnamese.

Alternatively, the children could be kept together, so that they spoke their own language, ate their own food, and followed the pattern of life they had left behind. This would probably cut them off from the people in the place where they were now living, making them homeless foreigners for the rest of their lives.

△ Many of the Vietnamese boat people who were lucky enough to survive the journey, were taken to Hong Kong where they waited to see if another country would accept them.

The way chosen by a Save the Children home just west of London was a success, and was followed by other host countries. At Hampton Court House the refugee children lived in family-sized groups and were cared for by Vietnamese adults.

△ These children went to live in the Save the Children home at Hampton Court in England, where they are well cared for.

They enjoyed the food, music, games and language of their old home, but went to local schools where they were helped to learn how to live in Britain.

When the first refugee children grew up, they left Hampton Court House to live independently, often with friends from their old and new homes. When two of them married, the mixture of wedding guests showed how much at home they had become.

△ At the home, the children did not lose touch with Vietnamese ways of living; familiar food was just as much fun, and an important reminder of their old home.

A FAMILY HOME

The threat of extreme danger forces families to leave home. Millions of people all over the world flee from their homes because they are threatened by natural disasters, such as flood or drought, or by war.

Refugees need food, and perhaps medicine, when they first reach safety. The first place of safety may be a well-organized refugee camp, if they are lucky. This might not be where the family wants to stay, but it is a place to stop and draw breath, to think about what has happened and to plan what to do next.

▽ After their escape to Nepal, these Tibetan refugees gradually begin to pick up the threads of an ordinary life once more. They have started to use their skills in spinning wool again.

When the Tibetans in the picture below first came to India, they went to a camp where they were given food and health checks. They were all fit, but they still needed help. The run to safety had made them very frightened and it was important that they all stayed together. As a family they were strong and able to cope with their situation.

The camp staff knew they must be given some kind of family home during their short stay. It could be a tent, or only sheets of plastic, but it would be their home for a while. Later, still together as families, these Tibetans moved on to a place of greater safety. Here each family started to put its life back together, and both parents and children could feel sure of belonging again.

△ Sudden disaster means that there is no time to prepare for refugees, but here in Colombia the Red Cross quickly provided tents to give proper shelter for these children.

This Bangladeshi girl, and 50,000 people like her, are not so lucky. The failure of important people to keep their promises means that there is no home, just misery and disease. ▷

SPLIT FAMILIES

Imagine a gigantic shed, big enough in which to play two or three football matches. The walls are plain brick, and there are very few windows. Now imagine this shed filled with beds, like an enormous dormitory. There are no curtains, no pictures – just long rows of beds. During the day, most of the beds are empty, but at night, people come back to sleep there. Think of the noise all these people would make.

This is what a 'mass shelter' in New York, or any one of the Western European countries, is like for people who have no other place to sleep.

In the USA there are over a quarter of a million people sleeping rough or in emergency shelters. Imagine a mother and her two children arriving at a shelter similar to the one on the right. This is what Mrs. Curran had to do.

Mrs Curran's husband had a good job as a truck driver. Just over a year ago he lost his job. He had done nothing wrong, but the company was not successful and did not need him anymore.

Without an income their savings were soon spent on rent and food and so they sold what they could to keep going. Then Mr Curran said there was no work in New York so he would try Chicago and send for them when he got a job. He left.

Birmingham is one of Britain's biggest cities, and has made great wealth for the country, but in this 'night shelter' the only hope for the homeless is that they will get some kind of bed in this huge dormitory. ▷

▽ A better kind of cardboard box has been made by an American architect; but it is not a home!

A month later the landlord threw Mrs Curran and her children out. Even with Josey and Joey to help, the family could not carry much away with them. This was probably just as well, because at the shelter they were only given two small steel lockers. Anything that could not be locked away, with really strong padlocks, was stolen.

Mrs Curran is afraid that Mr Curran might not come back or send for them. She is afraid that if he does he will not find them. She is afraid they will soon run out of money completely. Most of all she is afraid of what might happen to the children if they have to stay in a place like this. This is not a home.

▽ In America, unemployment can lead to families being separated as parents search for work.

HOME ON THE PAVEMENT

Lakshmi heard the train and knew it was time to get up. Soon the streets around the station in Calcutta would be crowded with people. She heard her mother moving, and knew her father had already gone to look for work.

▽ **In Calcutta, many homeless children find only one answer to their problems: live on the pavement.**

She rolled over on the pavement and shook her younger brother and sister awake. If they hurried they could get to the cold water tap before all the other 'pavement people' were awake. The tap was around the corner in the station yard, and was really for railway use. It was the only washing place for scores of people who slept on the streets nearby.

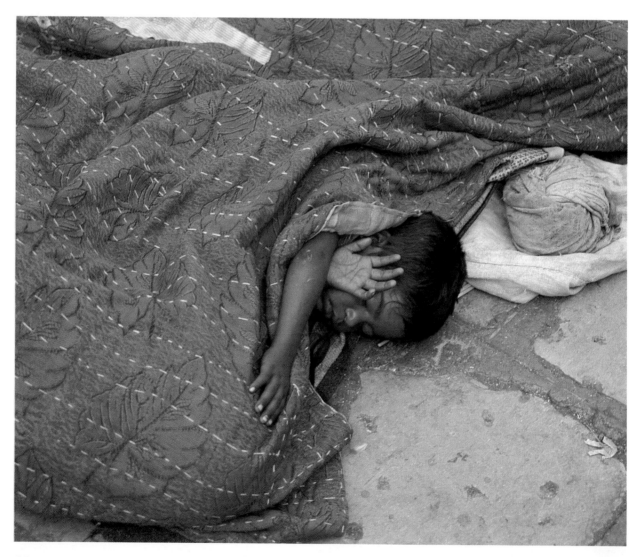

△ In Kampuchea, the same problem brings the same answer – even for proud and modest people.

Can you imagine trying to wash in a crowded street, with people milling around you? The people who live on the street have no choice. In Calcutta there is a great shortage of houses, and, as in other Indian cities, there are thousands of pavement people.

Sometimes it seemed to Lakshmi that they were invisible. Tourists, business people in a hurry, society ladies chatting as they went from taxi to train never seemed to notice them.

Quite often someone would give a few coins to a beggar, but they still did not see the beggar as a person, who had to eat, sleep and bring up children on the pavement by the station wall.

When charities brought the pavement people clothes, food or medicine, and took away the sick and dying, it made life a little easier for a while. At night Lakshmi often heard the younger adults talking about how they would change everything, but at dawn, in the hard reality of life, no one had any energy left from the struggle to survive from day to day.

MAKING A HOME

In Brazil there are many thousands of people who have been driven from their land. Families have had their homes knocked down, their crops burned and their lives threatened because rich and powerful men wanted their land. Even if they and their ancestors had lived on the land long before the new landowner came along, they were thrown out. Families live in fear of their lives because many people have been killed for resisting.

For poor farmers, no home means no food, because they have nowhere to grow their crops. Parents are afraid that their children will starve. When the land from which they have been driven is left unused, either while the landowners argue in court, or just because the landowner wants to keep it empty, the fear for the future of their children overcomes the fear of the bullies.

As a result, many of the landless people in Brazil have joined together in an organization called *Sem Terra*, to take over unused land for farming. In October 1985 one *Sem Terra* group of 8,000 people moved on to the 8,000 hectare Annoni farm in Rio Grande do Sul one night. Babies, children and adults with their tools, pots and pans, clothes and all their other belongings, were loaded on to lorries and driven to the farm. They managed to establish themselves before the police or anyone else could stop them.

The children play happily, but their parents worry: 'Can we stay here safely? Will even this be taken from us?' ▷

▽ This Brazilian demonstration has a message: the laws of land ownership must change.

They put up tents and rough shelters as people had done in more than 40 other *Sem Terra* camps in different areas of Brazil. They promised to support each other so that the families could have their own homes again. The next year, 250 of them marched over 480 km to the State Parliament in Porto Allegro and demanded to see the Minister for Land Reform. They won the support of the bishops – some church people had already been murdered for helping the landless – and then persuaded the Minister to promise 19,000 hectares of land for 1,500 families to make their home.

▽ In some parts of Brazil changes have been made, and homeless people have found a place to live, and a place to grow their crops.

HOME ON THE HILL

Jorge's back ached, his feet were sore, his hands were scratched and his legs were tired. But Jorge was happy.

How many times had he walked up the 100 m hill, carrying a cement block? They wouldn't let him make separate piles, so he lost count at five. His teenage brother and sister had longer legs and could run down the hill. Jorge kept pace with his mother, although she carried many more blocks than he did.

▽ **Around Rio de Janeiro in Brazil, every possible space is taken up. Here, Marta Hill favela covers the hillside with slums – better than nothing for the people who live there, but not much better.**

The house they were building was not going to be their home. Two more houses had to be built, before they began to work on their own home. Next month perhaps, they would have a new home. Jorge and his family were part of the new Co-operative Housing Scheme in Bahia, Brazil. It was called a co-operative because everybody worked on it and planned it together. None of the people who had moved from the shanty towns of the **favela** by the sea, had dropped out of the work once they had got their house. Even the old people did their share. Favela life had not taken away their sense of honour.

When they decided to build new houses, and shocked the city into giving them land, what a difference it made to those who had struggled with extreme poverty and homelessness for years. Jorge had seen the change begin when the grown-ups began the planning. Where would they go on the hillside? How big would each plot be? Who could do what work? How could they get supplies? People took on their duties with pride, and they called themselves the Nova Maratinho Housing Co-operative.

Everyone could see how successful they were. Now no one could push them around. Some had even found decent jobs. There were plans for a school and a clinic, and a nurse to teach them about hygiene.

Jorge felt happy. The fears he had had about the family breaking up disappeared. Instead, he dreamed about the new home that would soon be built on that terrace just up there.

△ (top) Jorge's house will be something like this. This new Brazilian village is the pride of the people who have made their own homes. They obtained the land and with a bit of help they bought the materials. They knew what they wanted – and together they succeeded.

△ In a self-help co-operation project, everybody works hard to see that all the families in the village get a new home. Even young people help out.

33

A PLACE TO MEET

Jamie ran. If he got to the Centre by 4 pm his mum would take him into the city for a new scarf, and he was keen to have it before Saturday's football match.

He wouldn't be afraid to wear it, either. The gangs did a lot less fighting now than a few years ago. Before the Centre and the café opened, Jamie's mum never let him come home from school on his own.

The estate where he and his family lived was better than the old **tenements** had been, but there was no real life going on there; 7,000 people were packed together with nothing much to do. Many of the adults were unemployed, some of the young people took drugs, and there was a lot of vandalism. Nobody seemed to know what to do about it.

The local council asked Save the Children to see what could be done. SCF thought that with enough government money the people on the estate could find some of their own answers to their problems. Jamie's mum had gone to the first meeting where the people on the estate could talk about the problems.

Mothers wanted somewhere safe where small children could play. Mothers with older children wanted a place where their children could go after school. That was where Jamie had to be by 4 pm – the Centre for mothers and children under twelve.

Children are nearly always happy to have their photographs taken, but there is not much else in a concrete jungle to make them happy. Who listens to what they want? ▷

His older sister went to the café. Instead of hanging about on street corners, she and her friends could get coffee and a bun there. Prices were kept low because local people volunteered to run the café.

Jamie's mum made sure he knew how lucky he was. She kept reminding him about what they had done together – the pantomime, the keep-fit classes, the coach trips – and the plans they still had.

Right now, Jamie's only plan was to get his scarf, and now he was on time they could go for the bus.

△ The Lewisham Council, in London, wants the local people to share in decisions about housing and other local needs, so the architect does not just work in his office, but outside where he can listen to people.

PORTAHOMES

Would you like to live in the same home but be able to move it to different places? Many families around the world have been doing that for generations. They keep herds or flocks of animals and have to move around to find water and new pasture. These people have to build movable homes. The children are a working part of a family like this. They help in the home and with the animals.

An Afghan home shows that a tent does not have to be plain or uncomfortable. This child is growing up in a home of great beauty.

Tribes of Native Americans, who lived on the plains until the end of the nineteenth century, relied on herds of buffalo for their food and clothing. Because the buffalo **migrated**, Native Americans made homes that they could carry with them. These homes, called tepees, were cone-shaped tents made of about seventeen buffalo hides. Some Native Americans in the USA and Canada still live in tepees, but they no longer live on the plains. Their land was taken from them by the white settlers who wanted to farm it.

△ A gypsy family in Rajasthan, India, is ready to move. They have not collected truck loads of belongings, but they have everything they need.

△ These tepees do not spoil the mountain view, and they have not used a great deal of natural materials, such as wood, to form a comfortable home.

The tribes that live on the **steppes** of Asia still rely on the **yak** for food, clothing and shelter. A yurt, a yak-hide tent, is a different shape to a tepee, and it suits the conditions of the climate.

The Arabs of North Africa are another nomadic people. They also need to follow their flocks of sheep and goats to new grazing land. The animals provide food, clothing and shelter as well. Arab traditions put a high value on hospitality, and a tent can be made very welcoming and luxurious. Arab tents are closer to yurts than to tepees in design.

HOMES OF GRASS

Grass has been used as a building material in countries all over the world for a long time. It makes a home warm and dry, particularly in tropical climates.

▽ In Zimbabwe, thatching grass is perfect to cover roofs. One man prepares each bundle of grass while another works on the roof. If they do the work well, the roof will keep out the worst storms.

In the past, people in Iceland grew grass on their roofs, and some Icelanders still do. When the slope is at just the right angle, the soil stays in place. The grass has strong roots and grows easily. There is no need to pay someone to repair the roof, no matter how fierce the winter is. Each family can look after its own roof.

Sometimes, in bad weather, Icelandic children hear about the troubles people have in blocks of flats or houses, and their parents say 'Here we are, warm and dry. Our grass roof keeps all the heat in. We are safe and comfortable. If only other people would learn.' Some other people have learned, and today's architects are planning new ways of using the old grass roofs on modern homes in Iceland.

Children in Zimbabwe in Africa, know that grass is used to cover roofs. After the rainy season each year, families and friends gather thatching grass at the riverside. At the end of an afternoon's work they walk back to the villages with great bundles of grass, nearly 2 m long, on their heads.

Very old houses in Iceland have green grass for their roofs. This style of building is now making a come-back. ▽

It takes a lot of grass to build a new house, so many people have to work hard at gathering it. When the roof timbers are in place, small bundles of grass are set in position. At the same time, older roofs are patched. When winter comes, the houses will be warm. When summer comes, with temperatures as high as 40°C, the houses will be cool and the rain will be kept out, without the clatter it would make on an expensive iron roof.

These houses in Brazil also use thatching for roofs. They are set in neat rows, but their local materials make them very different from rows of houses in big industrial cities. ▽

TRAVELLING PEOPLE

Gypsies are special people. They have their own language and many of their own customs. Centuries ago they travelled westwards from India and spread across Europe. In each country some stayed, but some always moved on to new places, looking for work and somewhere to stay for a while. Today they do not have the same traditional caravans, but they still travel around.

▽ Gypsy caravans are very comfortable to live in. Everything is spotlessly clean and close at hand.

People often fear, or dislike, people or things that they are not familiar with. In less serious ways, this can affect one's taste in clothing or food and drink, for example. More dangerously, it affects people's judgement about other people. Gypsies have often been feared, and even hated. In Hitler's Nazi Germany in the early 1940s they were sent to **concentration camps** and killed. In Spain, where there are about half a million gypsies living in poor housing, they are often hurt in racist attacks.

In Britain, they are treated in a variety of ways. There are many old stories of 'Romany' ways which make gypsy life seem romantic and attractive, but there are other stories which make gypsies seem a threat to other people.

However, everyone agrees that gypsy children should have a good start in life, so special teachers are provided for them. Local councils have to provide good sites, by law, where gypsies can park their caravans. There should be clean water, drains and all necessary services. Although everyone seems to agree that these gypsy sites are necessary, no one seems to want such a site near them.

△ This site at Gainsborough is properly equipped and can be kept clean and tidy. Too often the sites set aside for travelling people are so bad to start with that no one could take pride in living there.

People do not have real reasons for refusing, but the fear of something or someone strange is quite enough.

Every year, somewhere in Britain, there is a burst of anger and fear in local newspapers and council offices, and a group of gypsies is told it is not welcome. Each year a few more gypsies give up their travelling life and their caravans and move into houses for the sake of their children.

EARTH AS OUR HOME

This book will go into homes and schools in many parts of the world. In any town where it is read, there will be someone in every school who covers their notebook or file with a long, long address which ends up with *earth, solar system, universe*, and even more if they can think of it.

Our home together is the earth, the third planet from the sun. We all share the same balance of gases in the air, we need the same water and food for health and the same force of gravity controls our growth.

▽ **Danger lies in the bubbles of the river. This is not clean water; it has been polluted by detergent.**

We all want our home to be clean and well stocked with food. We want to be free to enjoy the food and to live happy lives. Within this big home, we all want more or less the same for our small homes. We all have a share in making sure it is possible, just as in each small home we share in making the home good or bad.

In the world, some people do not really enjoy life because others are selfish or greedy. These people not only spoil the earth for everybody else, they spoil it for themselves, but do not seem to see it. We must make sure that our earth is not spoiled. We must look to the future, and remember the generations to follow.

△ When pictures from space first showed earth as a ball, the beautiful blue of it brightened millions of homes. The earth is home for all of us and we must keep it clean and thriving with healthy life.

GLOSSARY

Asylum A place of safety; by international agreement, when refugees look for asylum, the country to which they go has to allow them certain rights of entry and cannot just refuse entry or send them back into danger.

Civil War A war in which the people of one country fight against each other, and not against another country.

Concentration camp A prison camp for prisoners of war or people seen as enemies of a country. Millions of people died in such camps in Nazi Germany during the Second World War (1939–45).

Deport To send someone out of the country, making it illegal for them to return.

Developing countries Poorer countries which do not yet have the housing, work opportunities, education or health care that rich countries, or developed countries, take for granted.

Euston Station A major railway terminus in London, serving travellers from the Midlands and the North. When the station was re-designed some years ago, the benches and chairs which had previously been used by homeless people to sleep on under cover were not included.

Exiles People who are forced to flee and remain away from their own country.

Favela A **slum** in Brazil, often near the water's edge or by a river.

Guerrilla war A war in which small bands of soldiers attack a large army. In Sri Lanka, for example, the Tamils are fighting a guerrilla war against the Sri Lankan government forces.

Gypsies Groups of people who live and travel through much of Europe. They have their own language and customs, and the name comes from an old tradition that they originally came from Egypt. It is more likely that they came from India, centuries ago.

Literacy The ability to read and write.

Migrate To move from one place to another, often depending on the season.

Mortgage A special loan which enables someone to buy a house.

Physiotherapist A medical specialist who gives care to people with physical disabilities – often by teaching them exercises to strengthen or flex their limbs.

Policies Plans made by a government to follow, such as a housing policy.

Racism Being unpleasant or violent towards members of another race; believing your own race to be better than any other.

Refuge A place of temporary safety from danger. The name has been used for shelters for 'battered wives' who have had to escape from violence at home.

Refugees People who have to leave home to find safety for a while, from dangers such as flood, famine or invasion.

Sanctuary A safe place for someone running away from danger or ill-treatment. In the past, if someone sought sanctuary in a church, no one was allowed to harm them, no matter what they had done.

Slum An area of very bad housing where basic facilities, such as drains and a fresh water supply, are of a poor standard. It can also describe a single house.

Steppes Large plains, usually without trees.

Unemployment Being unable to find work.

Yak An animal like an ox found in Tibet.

TEACHERS' NOTES

HOME is an emotive subject, and must be handled carefully, but it is also one which lends itself to some degree of objective study (see book list on page 45). Children are not responsible for their own housing, and any comparisons must not introduce a sense of judgement. Homes are a universal need, and involvement in a sympathetic consideration of how families live can help in overcoming some cultural or racial prejudices.

The best approach to the subject is a positive one. It is right to celebrate human care and ingenuity, and the ability to rise above many dangers. The real enjoyment of a home can be appreciated across cultural boundaries, and the stories of need in this book are intended to emphasize the self-reliance of people when they receive even minimal support or are relieved from pressures, often political. Not all cases can have a happy ending, and so several of these stories leave the position unresolved.

Every nation has its own homeless people. This fact should make it impossible for any nation to view the failure of others to care for their needy as a sign of inferiority. No one has solved the problem of the quality of life, but it is not unreasonable to take the level of national or regional wealth into account when considering what could be done and what has been achieved.

Similarly, every continent has its refugees and exiles; many of the worst situations have their roots in the selfish interests of externals powers. In recent years, there has been an increasingly obvious reluctance to meet the basic duties of asylum and hospitality for refugees.

For 1987, the International Year of Shelter for the Homeless, the United Nations produced criteria which real homes must reach. In addition to protection from the elements, a home must offer basic services and facilities, security, accessibility and affordability.

These criteria seem to reflect the viewpoint of a modern, industrial, settled society, and some of the details may be disputed by people who find personal fulfilment and cultural satisfaction in some of the home-styles mentioned in this book. Although urbanization is a global phenomenon, it will not be until the next century that half the world's population will be living in cities – the forecast is 54 per cent by 2010. Whether, for example, an Amazonian Indian should be forced into housing which would meet legal housing standards in Britain is an argument which is beyond the scope of this book, but is perhaps approachable in a class discussion.

The basic level of services and facilities required includes piped water, toilets, (or equivalent disposal system), garbage disposal, site drainage, access roads, emergency services and, where possible, electricity. It is clear from this that the key quality of a home, as identified by the UN, is closely concerned with health and hygiene, including community health. The International Decade for Water which concentrated on the provision of clean water and effective sewage disposal, was unsuccessful. This puts a big question mark against the understanding of what could be achieved by those governments which approved the IYSH criteria.

Security of tenure affects both owners and tenants, and requires not only satisfactory laws but also access to those laws and reliable enforcement procedures. Security may also be linked to income – anyone who has to pay so much for housing that food, health, and education are out of reach, may have little security, even without the additional danger of unmanageable debts.

The quality of life is also related to the accessibility of health centres, schools and places of work. The free decision to undertake daily commuting to work should be distinguished from a legal requirement to spend four or more hours a day travelling, because the 'dormitory areas' are remote from employment, as in South Africa.

More than a quarter of the world's population, approximately 4,000,000,000 people, is deprived of 'shelter' which meets all four criteria; they are 'homeless'. In school it may be useful to consider whether a broken family in a mass shelter, and an extended nomadic family living in a hide tent, are equally homeless in human terms.

Comparisons may also be made between the experiences of solitary homeless people in the rich cities of the developed world, the families which live on the streets in India – 100,000 pavement dwellers in Bombay alone – and the children without any family support who survive on the streets of many Latin American cities (uncounted, but certainly numbering tens of millions). Expectations may be taken into account, together with the degree of responsibility accepted by authorities and charities.

BOOKS TO READ

Children's Further Reading

A History of Building Materials by N. Davey, (Phoenix House, 1961).

A Look at Homes by M. Crush, (Franklin Watts, 1971).

Away from The Bright Lights by A. Wiggins and the Greater Manchester Youth Association, (CHAR, 1982).

Homes in Cold Places by A. James, (Wayland, 1987).

Homes in Hot Places by A. James, (Wayland, 1987).

Houses and Homes by C. Bowyer, (Usborne Publishing, 1978).

Houses and Homes by C. Cocke, (Macdonald Educational, 1976).

Houses and Homes by H. Kurth, (World's Work Ltd, 1980).

Houses and Homes Around the World by J. Karavasil, (Macmillan, 1983).

Adult Resource Material

A Time to Build: People's Housing in Asia by J. Anzorena and W. Poussard, (IYSH, 1987)

Capital Decay, (SHAC, 1986).

Cities, Poverty and Development: Urbanization in the Third World by A. G. Gilbert and J. Gugler, (Oxford University Press, 1982).

Doorways, (IYSH, 1987).

Handbook of Housing for the Disabled by J. Penton and A. Barlow, (London Housing Consortium, 1980).

Housing, (Centre for World Development Education, 1987).

Housing Co-operatives in Developing Countries by A. C. Lewin, (Plunkett Foundation, 1981).

Housing in Multi-Racial Areas, (Commission for Racial Equality, 1984).

Not Just a Roof by J. Gilbert, (CHAR, 1986).

USEFUL ADDRESSES

Many organizations produce useful teachers' materials on housing and homelessness in developed and developing countries.

Barnardo's Homes, Tanners Lane, Barkingside, Ilford, Essex IG6 1QG.

Child Poverty Action Group, 4th Floor, 1–5 Bath Street, London EC1V 9TY.

Christian Aid, PO Box No 1, London SW9 8BH.

Cyrenians (Home for Homeless People) 4th Floor, Smithfield House, Digbeth, Birmingham B5 6BS.

Department of the Environment, 2 Marsham Street, London SW1P 3EB.

Housing Campaign for Single People (CHAR), 5–15 Cromer Street, London WC1H 8LS.

Housing Centre Trust, 33 Alfred Place, London WC1E 7JU.

International Year of Shelter for the Homeless '87, 8th Floor, 19–29 Woburn Place, London WC1H OLY.

Leaving Home Project, 5 Egmont House, 116 Shaftesbury Avenue, London W1V 7DJ.

National Children's Home, 85 Highbury Park, London N5 1UD.

National Federation of Housing Associations, 175 Grays Inn Road, London WC1X 8UP.

Royal Institute of British Architects (RIBA) 66 Portland Place, London W1N 4AD.

Save the Children, Mary Datchelor House, 17 Grove Lane, London SE5 8RD.

Shelter, 157 Waterloo Road, London SE1 8XF.

Single Homeless Project, 16–18 Strutton Ground, London SW1P 2HP.

Women's Aid Federation, 374 Featherstone Street, London EC1.

Young Homelessness Group, 169 Clapham Road, London SW9 OPU.

Material should also be available nationally from Building Societies, who offer information on housing, and from the 'Social Responsibility' Departments of the major Churches. Local information should be available from Local History Societies and Museums, the Housing Departments of Local Authorities, Citizens Advice Bureaux, and offices of the Probation and After Care Services.

PICTURE CREDITS

INDEX

Page numbers that refer to pictures are in **bold**.